Smelf the
The Town of Vidsville

Les Anas

Copyright © 2019 Les Anas
All rights reserved.
ISBN: 9781086762013

DEDICATION

This book is dedicated to my mother. May she rest in peace.

Smelf is a happy little elf.

CJ walks down the street.

Grandpa drives past in a red tractor.

CJ loves to sing holiday carols.

He is in front of the toy store.

CJ looks on the ground.

He finds a ten dollar bill.

He wants to buy a toy.

Smelf looks out the window.

Smelf runs out to hide.

CJ walks down the street.

Smelf throws magic sprinkles.

Smelf giggles and runs away.

A friend drives past in a dump truck.

CJ sees Santa ringing a bell.

CJ wants to donate the money he found.

CJ puts the money in the bucket.

The man thanks CJ for the donation.

CJ wishes him happy holidays.

He walks down the street.

CJ is very happy.

Many people were happy because of that one little elf.
Smelf the Elf

ABOUT THE AUTHOR

Les Anas has been creating videos and short stories for children for over ten years. Creativity and making children laugh is his lifelong passion.

Made in the USA
Monee, IL
29 November 2024

71666351R00017